Boats

by
Gail Saunders-Smith

Pebble Books
an imprint of Capstone Press

Pebble Books

Pebble Books are published by Capstone Press
818 North Willow Street, Mankato, Minnesota 56001
http://www.capstone-press.com
Copyright © 1998 by Capstone Press
All Rights Reserved • Printed in the United States of America

Library of Congress Cataloging-in-Publication Data
Saunders-Smith, Gail.
  Boats/by Gail Saunders-Smith.
  p. cm.
  Includes bibliographical references (p. 23) and index.
  Summary: Simple text and photographs introduce the
reader to many types of boats and ships, including canoes,
paddle wheels, and aircraft carriers.
  ISBN 1-56065-497-X
  1. Boats and boating--Juvenile literature. [1. Boats and
boating. 2. Ships.] I. Title.

VM150.S325 1997
623.8--DC21
                        97-23583
                         CIP
                         AC

Editorial Credits
Lois Wallentine, editor; Timothy Halldin and James Franklin, design;
Michelle L. Norstad, photo research

Photo Credits
International Stock/Peter Langone, cover
Mark Turner, 10
Unicorn Stock/H.H. Thomas, 8; Karen Holsinger Mullen, 12;
  Alice M. Prescott, 1, 16
U.S. Navy, 20
Valan Photos/Phil Norton, 4; Tom W. Parkin, 6; Jean Bruneau, 14
George White Location Photography, 18

Table of Contents

A canoe is a boat
that can work
on a river.

A kayak is a boat
that can work
on a river.

A paddle wheeler is a boat that can work on a river.

A sailboat is a boat
that can work
on a lake.

A rowboat is a boat
that can work
on a lake.

A motorboat is a
boat that can work
on a lake.

A tugboat is a boat
that can work
on the ocean.

A cruise ship is a
ship that works
on the ocean.

An aircraft carrier is
a ship that works
on the ocean.

Words to Know

aircraft carrier—a large, flat ship where airplanes and jets can land

canoe—a small, shallow boat that people move through water with paddles

cruise ship—a large ship that people travel on for a vacation

kayak—a small, enclosed boat for one person that is moved with a paddle

motorboat—a fast, medium-sized boat that is moved by a motor

paddle wheeler—a large riverboat that is moved by a spinning wheel

rowboat—a small boat that people move through water with oars

sailboat—a small or large boat that moves by catching wind in its sails

tugboat—a small, powerful boat that pulls or pushes ships

Read More

Asimov, Isaac and Elizabeth Kaplan. *How Do Big Ships Float?* Milwaukee: Gareth Stevens Publishing, 1993.

Davies, Kay and Wendy Oldfield. *My Boat.* Milwaukee: Gareth Stevens Publishing, 1994.

Lincoln, Margarette. *Amazing Boats.* New York: Alfred A. Knopf, 1992.

Internet Sites

Kids-'n-Boating
http://catalog.com/bobpone/kids.htm

Nick's Kayak Page
http://www.guillemot-kayaks.com/Kayak.html

Note to Parents and Teachers

This book describes various types of boats and ships. The book also introduces three different bodies of water. The photographs clearly illustrate the text and support the child in making meaning from the words. Children may need assistance in using the Table of Contents, Words to Know, Read More, Internet Sites, and Index/Word List sections of the book.

Index/Word List

Word Count: 100